F*ck You With My Words

Erin Hyvonen

Presentation by *BookLeaf Publishing*

Web: www.bookleafpub.com

E-mail: info@bookleafpub.com

ISBN: 9789357214070

First edition 2023

*I would love to thank my followers. I write
about sex because it's real and it's an important
part of life. Sex is an act of love we create with
the person that we care about. May my words
bring you happiness and pleasure.*

ACKNOWLEDGEMENT

To my family and friends, thank you for your love and support in my life.
To Joe Broderick, for your inspiration and motivation in writing, and working with me.

PREFACE

To all the lovers out there. I hope my poems inspire you to be creative and to have fun with your partner! May they help you create passionate times for you and your lover. And Now, I proudly present my erotic poetry.

Baby, I'm Yours Tonight.

I want to make you mine.
Now remove all of your clothes
Let's be nude in the moonlight.
Surrounded by candle lights.
Baby I'm yours tonight.
I've set the mood for me and you.
I got lots of body oil to spoil you.
Feel me massage you.
Just to relax you.
Cuddle and touch you.
Baby I'll be gentle and smooth.
I love having my hands on you.
Just looking at you and your body.
Holding you in so tightly.
Hugging you so nicely.
Kissing you so fondly.
Looking into your eyes.
Watching you smile.
Baby I'm yours tonight.

I'm in charge.

Relax for me baby.
Hold up your hands.
I'm up for some bondage.
Let me bound and blindfold you.
Make sure your comfortable.
Cause you cannot move.
I'm in charge of you.
Do you trust me?
Do I dare?
Make you flutter and shiver.
While I'll caress your body
with a feather.
Take a breather and
Experience your senses.
Open your mouth.
Let me put in
something sweet to eat with.
Kiss you so deliciously.
Stroke your lips with my fingers.
Tease you so slowly.
Take my time with kisses.
All over your neck.
Make you gasp for more.
While I got a hold of you.
Your in my control.

Let me grop you fondly.
Rub you so nicely.
Feel your beautiful body.
I'm touching you tonight.
You're my prize
and I'm going to take my time.
Smell this let the aroma enter your nose.
It's just a sweet smelling rose.
Feel the petals on your skin.
While we have some fun with it.
Now get ready
cause it's gonna be a shock.
It starts off all wet and cold.
Got a few ice cubes crushed in my mouth.
Sucking all of your sensitive spots.
While it sends you to a rush.
Till its all warm and melts in my mouth.
Baby I just want you to cum.
Tell me now what you want me to do.
How can I relieve you.

Let's get down tonight.

Love you too.
I like you lots.
You make me so hot.
I flare up.
I just want to jump on top of you.
Ride you so good.
Make you in the mood.
Move your pelvis in a rhythmic groove.
While you caress my boobs.
Make me feel so good.
Cum all over you.
Bend me over.
Take me from behind.
Have a good time.
Let's get down tonight.

I just want to make love to you.

I just want to make love to you.
Hold you tight.
In my arms tonight.
My breasts press against your chest.
My legs wrap around your waist.
Thrust inside me.
Slow and deep.
Keep it this rythum.
And look into my eyes.
Kiss me.
Nipple on my ear.
Tell me things I want to hear.
Like that I am sexy and sweet.
Feel me squeezing
While you penetrate me.
In so deep.
Hitting my g spot.
Getting me to cum alot.
I'm begging for more.
I want you all.
Take it till I explode.
Having multiples.

Devouring You

How much I want to be on my knees.
In front of you.
Devouring you.
Planting kisses with my lips.
Flicking my tongue along your skin.
I want you to shiver and moan.
Hold my head in tight.
While I make you cum tonight.
Grap my hair pull me in closer.
My whole mouth open wide.
All for You, On You.
Suck on your bits.
While I flick my tongue in.
Groan and rock your pelvis in.
Sweat and feel the heat kick in.
Shake for me baby.
Have multiple orgasms.
Come again and again.
Let the juice drip out from within.
Catch your breath.
Now…Lets cuddle
and embrace this moment.
Of contentment.
Satisfaction.

Desires.

My tongue desires to devour you.
Taste your juices.
Kiss you.
All the way.
My mouth desires to pash you.
Touch your lips.
Caress you with my tongue.
Make out with you all day long.
Have my hands all over you.
Have my body pressed against you.
Have some heavy petting.
Getting heated.
How much I want to strip off your clothing.
Have you expose and vulnerable.
Naked and beautiful.
How I want to rub your privates.
Get real close and comfortable.
Enjoy the moment.
Groan and moan.
Cum hard now.

I'm so fine, fuck you tonight.

Long legs, nice and smooth to touch with.
Long hair, smells so good.
Big boobs, so cute with the cleavage.
Clean pussy, so wet so yummy to eat.
Big butt, tight asshole to fuck.
Big lips, plenty to kiss.
Long tongue, slip that along your skin.
Long arms, wrap you up in.
Big eyes, stare at you all times.
I'm so fine, I wanna make you mine.
Wine and dine.
Fuck you all the time.
Let's do a 69.
Make me cum a few times.
Stick it in my hole.
I'm in the mood for anal.
I'll rub myself while you're penetrating me.
Make me squirt with your fingers.
When you press on my g spot.
I'll come multiple times cause I have a high sex
drive.
I'm not shy in sexuality.
I'll dig in and give you a good lick.
Sit on my face.

I'll suck your balls and cock so good Make you
move in a rhythm while you fuck my face.
Pull out and jizz on me tits.

Pleasing me.

Having thoughts of sneaking rubs.
I just can't get enough.
I'm so hot.
My Kundalini energies are running through my
sacral.
My clitoris begging to be touch.
I want it so much.
In private I go.
Take my pants off.
Bring my hand down below.
Put my fingers down between my legs.
Rub myself in a motion.
My hips swaying.
My body presses against my hand.
Each pressure I'm getting pleasure.
I know how to please me.
How to give my body what I need.
To relieve me from my cravings.

Give me your cock.

Just give me your cock.
I want to suck it so much.
Just get Infront if me.
Take your pants off.
Let me see it.
I want to touch you with my hands.
Give you a good rub.
Hold your cock.
Feel it's touch.
Put it in mouth.
I dare you to do it.
I wanna feel it on my tongue.
Slide it in.
Let me suck on it.
Press it in with my lips.
Suck gently on your tip.
Pull my hair I dare you.
Get a grip and move my head.
I want you to let loose.
Let me devour you.
Make you all wet and sensitive.
Begging me not to stop doing it.
Let me explore your balls with my tongue and
mouth.
I want to taste you so much.

I'll give you so much attention.
I want to send you to heaven.
I want to build you up and make you explode.

Be my submissive.

So dominant I'll tell you what to do.
Be my submissive and give in to my requests.
Go down on me and lick my ass out.
Give my clit attention and
Start fingering my asshole.
Lay down I want to climb on top of you
Position your cock near my hole.
I'm going to start out slow.
Has it's so tight in the asshole.
Don't move let me fuck you.
Just keep sucking my boobs.
While I slowly stick this cock in.
Bit by bit
While im rubbing my clit.
I'm so relaxed its getting deeper in.
I'm getting all excited over it
The thrill of your cock deep in my rear.
The feeling of the penetrating when I move up
the tempo.
Bouncing up and down at a pace.
My head is off in space.
Telling you I'm close to climaxing.
Telling you to cum in my ass.
Telling you I'm cumming so hard.
You take over and pump out your load.
Now wasn't that fun for us.

Smack that.

I love my big butt I cannot deny.
Want you to smack that.
Smack it so more.
Make me sore.
Let's bring out the paddle.
Smack me in the middle of riding your dick.
Create the distraction while im trying to have orgasms.
Grab my butt and pull down on me so deep.
Go behind me.
Let's do doggy.
Hold my hips and thrust in slowly.
Keep teasing me.
Make me beg for your dick to go fully in.
Take it slow.
Make me beg for more.
Keep smacking my bottom some more.
Tell me I'm your naughty girl.
Keep penetrating me.
I'm so hungry for a release.
It's building up inside me.
I'm full of heat.
I'm ready to explode.
Pull out and let your juice drip all over my body.

Lay Beside Me.

I'm so horny.
Lay beside me.
Put my undies to the side.
Rub me.
Rub my pussy now.
Finger me.
Touch my boobies.
Kiss me passionately.
I love it when you give attention to my neck.
Lick my earlobes.
Whisper me dirty things.
Like what you want to do to me.
Slide your cock in.
Let me move my hips.
Lets get into the rhythm of it.
Your cock so hard for me.
I'm full of moist.
Lets cum together and make
some noise.

Cunnilingus.

Spread those legs.
Lick your thighs.
Time to eat your pussy out tonight.
Make you squirm.
Sit on my face.
Let me taste your nectar flavour.
Rub yourself on my chin.
While I'll lick your clit.
Suck on your lips.
Kiss your bits.
Cum for me baby in bliss.
Move your hips.
Get real into it.
Rock your body side to side.
Get real high.

Party at my place tonight.

Lets get high.
Party at my place tonight.
Let's have fun and smoke up a storm. Get all
comfortable.
Take off our clothes we go.
Let's hang out in the nude.
I want to seduce you.
Come lick me out.
I want your tongue now.
Make me beg for you to stick it in.
Tease me and play with me just a little bit.
Glide your tongue along my vulva before you
enter my vagina.
Come put your penis in me so deep.
Keep teasing me.
Give my breasts some attention.
Nibble those nipples.
Flick your tongue around them while your
fucking me.
Make me pant.
Make me gasp for more.
Let me dirty talk.
Let me cry out to god.
Let me moan.
Let me grasp for air when we've cum.

Adult Shop.

I'll take you to the adult shop.
Go pick something exclusive.
It's all X rated.
Enjoyment for me and you.
What do you fancy?
What are you into?
Theres bondage.
Anal and dildo equipment.
Straps on and lube.
Vibrators and cock rings too.
Theres handcuffs, whips and buckles.
For the submissive.
We got pornographic magazines and video
content.
What's your vision?
There's dress up stuff and body paint.
What's your flavour?
There's games and quests.
What's your favourite?
Massage oils and feather sticks.
Dirty dice and paddle sticks.
What takes your interest?

Craving Intimacy.

I'm so hot.
Flames between my legs.
I'm building up kundalini energies in a circuit.
It's running through my sacral to my pelvic.
My clitoris is feeling the heat.
My body is craving intimacy.
I want to have fun and put on a show.
Wear some sexy lingerie.
Put on a pose.
Do a dance.
Some tantric rituals.
Bring out the candles and the satin sheets.
We are going to be romantic.

I'm your lover.

I'm your lover.
I'll surrender.
I'm devoted to you.
Giving you all my attention.
Giving you lots of affection.
Flirting with you.
I'll be your safe place.
Your sense of security.
I'll be everything you need me to be.
I'll fulfill your fantasies.
Your wishes.
Your dreams.
Dress up and play the role just for you.
Take my time with foreplay.
Explore your body and listen to you breathe.
Read your body language.
Telling me how to please.
Tell me how you like it.
What do you want me to do.
It's all about pleasuring you.
Cherishing you with my love.
I love you so much.

I crave you.

I ache to touch your lips.
With a kiss.
I crave your intimacy.
You give me these feelings.
I crave to touch your body.
Make out in ecstasy.
Loving you so deeply.
Yet so passionately.
I wanna get real close.
And get real tight.
Have you all to myself tonight.
Your my flavour.
I cannot get enough.
Your my favourite.
Your the only one I want to be with.
Your like Honey.
All so sweet.
You'll have me on my knees.
Between your legs.
Making you go all jelly.
Loving your body.
Fondling you.
Being all naughty.
Let's become one.
Hit the right spot.

Make us cum.
Enjoy the waves of an orgasm.
Sending us to heaven.
Have a breather.
And lay back to our hearts beating.
Cuddling and taking it all in.

Cyber Sex.

You keep messaging me for a booty call.
You keep sending me those naughty emojis.
Your so in the nasty mood.
Sending me those nudes.
Wanna get wet.
Wanna have cyber sex.
Posing.
Taking selfies.
Telling me what you want to do to me.
Telling me all your dirty stories.
Having fun masterbating.
Tell me how you want it.
Using your words.
I want to know what is your
fantasy?
What are you dreaming?
It's getting me so hot and worked up.
I love how we talk so hot.
Photos exchanging.
Doing some filming.
My body temperature is rising.
I'm close to cumming.
Im watching your recordings.
Your telling me how much you want me.
It's so exciting.

Return the favour.

Make you sing.
Make you groan for more.
While I deep throat your hard on.
Do my magic.
Make my mouth work.
Up and down.
And all around your manhood.
Cum for me baby.
Make a squirt.
All down my t shirt.
Now it's time to return the favour.
Get down there and start to
devour my cunt.
Lick it all up.
Suck on my bits.
Curl your tongue on my clit.
Kiss and suck those lips.
Finger both my holes.
Make me cum real hardcore.

www.ingramcontent.com/pod-product-compliance
Lightning Source LLC
La Vergne TN
LVHW051246200726
843510LV00011B/1710